TEACH ME HOW TO DIE

TO HELP THE TERMINALLY ILL TO TAKE CHARGE OF THE LAST DAYS

CALVIN E. RAINS, SR.

Bloomington, IN  Milton Keynes, UK

AuthorHouse™
1663 Liberty Drive, Suite 200
Bloomington, IN 47403
www.authorhouse.com
Phone: 1-800-839-8640

AuthorHouse™ UK Ltd.
500 Avebury Boulevard
Central Milton Keynes, MK9 2BE
www.authorhouse.co.uk
Phone: 08001974150

First published by AuthorHouse 4/11/2006

ISBN: 1-4259-2422-0 (sc)

Library of Congress Control Number: 2006902313

*Printed in the United States of America
Bloomington, Indiana*

This book is printed on acid-free paper.

ACKNOWLEDGEMENTS

I want to dedicate this book primarily to the young man who asked me to teach him how to die. He opened to me a door of opportunity and for all that will take time to walk with those who are terminally ill. To be asked to walk with a dying person in their last journey is a great privilege. Every step taken is on sacred ground.

I also dedicate this book to my wife and my family who have helped me beyond measure to face the last days of my own life. I also thank all those who prayed for me and did so many visible efforts of support. I offer special thanks to the eighty plus persons in twelve states who walked with me by e-mail as Prayer Partners in my struggle with Pancreatic Cancer. God will repay. I am also grateful to Randy and Dottie Robertson for encouraging me and helping me to get to a publisher.

Contents

INTRODUCTION

This book is not about suicide, assisted or other-wise. This effort is addressed to those who have been informed, or they believe, they have a terminal illness and the time is short. Suicide is most often a crime against those whom you leave behind. This effort is a gift of love.

This is an effort to help the dying plan the last days in a way to serve as a picture frame around the way they lived the rest of their lives. Our final days are the bottom line to all the other days we lived. What we communicate to those around us in our death will have a greater impact that what we said or did in the rest of our life.

Why not make the ending our own? We had no con-trol over our beginning. We had limited control over our youth. As we grew older we grew in our ability to make decisions about where we lived and what we did with most of our time. In our youth we tested the authority around us. In the working years of our lives we lived within that authority.

Now, as we face a death we did not choose, we must not think we have no control over the end of our lives. Within limitations, we can live these last days in our own way. We must decide to do it our way. Others will try to help by planning for you. You must be in control of that help

This book is intended to help the terminally ill take charge of their life and to live the last part in the most fulfilling way possible. It is to help, in so far as is possible, to control the content and events of those last days. It is also intended to be a guide for the caregivers who walk with the terminally ill. The caregiver needs to help the patient discover what is possible. It is one thing to just accept what others want for you in your last opportunities. It is another wonderful possibility to take control and to experience some quality time as you chart your own course. Either choice will lead to the same end, but within limits, you can decide how to get there.

It is readily admitted that there are circumstances present in many terminal illnesses that may limit what can be done. There may be physical limitations. Some terminal illnesses take charge of part or all of the physical body limiting our ability to control our activities. Sometimes the loss of physical control is gradual. Sometimes it is sudden and without warning.

Most often, within every circumstance, there are opportunities for the patient to give guidance to those who minister. Sometimes there may be a communication barrier. Discover your limitations and reach out. This book is to challenge you to do it your way.

CHAPTER I

UNDERSTANDING DEATH

Dying is a fact of life. You cannot have life without death. It is an accepted fact that all living things will die sometime, somehow, somewhere. We have a lot of choices as to how we arrive at the end, but we never control it all. Many things are not within our control. In our working years most of us worked in an environment controlled by someone else. We did work prescribed by our job description. Within our total day we did have some hours in which we could make decisions. This was non-job-related time within our control. During this time we took vacations and work breaks from time to time. But a large part of our lives was shaped by circumstances beyond our control. From the time we are born we are controlled by others, at least to some degree.

We live on a dying earth that is surrounded by a dying universe. New life springs forth around us every day. Other things die. New life is born. This will continue to be the cycle until the end of time when all things will die. This is not just a religion concept, scientist have the same convictions.

We must learn to take a lesson from the trees that lose their leaves every fall. The last days of the leaves are more beautiful and noticeable above all the days before. A variety of colors spring forth to call attention to the trees they adorn. Each kind of tree has its own way of calling attention to its presence. People drive hundreds of miles to see the wonderful fall colors of the trees in the mountains.

We can do the same with our lives. We can make the last days mean more than all the rest. At least we can use the last days under our control to call attention to those things we considered most important along the way of life. We can rebuild weakened relationships. We can reach out to friends to express appreciation for friendship. We can leave this life with all things in their best order. It is desired by this writer that when that final chapter comes each individual can say with a smile, "that is my final statement, I did it my way."

The motivation for this book came a few years ago when I had a 28-year-old young man of my congregation in the hospital. The family said they did not know what was wrong with him. I heard a rumor that he had AIDS. I went to see him. As soon as I walked into his room, he told me he had AIDS. He was convinced that he was dying. We discussed his illness for a few minutes, and then he said, "You spend a lot of time teach-

ing people how to live. Can you teach me how to die?"
Never before had I been challenged this way.

How this young man came into my life seemed to
be an act of God. His family joined my church one
Sunday telling me they had known me before in California. This came about while I was a Navy Chaplain
stationed at Naval Air Station, San Diego. Each Sunday
morning I went to a small air station near the border of
Mexico. I held an early service and then went to a civil-
ian church near San Diego to join my wife and children
in worship. Since I was coming from a military worship
service, I wore my uniform and was easily noticed as I
worshipped.

The mother of this young man married the son of
the pastor of that church. I did not get to know them at
that time. As time passed I went on to Korea as Chaplain with the First Marine Division. This family later
decided to leave California to escape some groups with
which youth were involved. Evidently they did not leave
soon enough. This young man was involved with drugs
and women. Eventually AIDS took hold of his life.

The young man's challenge brought back memories
of a discussion I had some years before with a physician
friend. He challenged me by suggesting that ministers
did not prepare the terminally ill to deal with death.
My response then was that most families did not want
to talk about death as long as there was life. I told him
of one middle-aged woman who was dying of cancer.
Her family instructed me that I was not to mention
neither death nor her illness. For weeks I made regular
visits to this lady in the hospital. I honored the wishes

of the family. I never mentioned the possibility of death and we did not speak directly of her cancer. However, I discovered very quickly that the lady knew she was dying and she was aware of the nature of her illness. We just never used the forbidden words. We were able to have meaningful conversations without using the key words.

I took this young man's challenge seriously and did the best I could to help him face each phase of his dying. I tried to help him make choices that shaped the content of his last days. I wanted him to be in charge, but I was there to help him evaluate his possibilities. I was able to enlist the members of his family in meaningful relationships. He taught me much more than I taught him. His challenge helped **shape** the last years of my ministry.

What I learned walking toward death with this friend reinforced what I had learned from a dying schoolteacher some years before. As her pastor, this wonderful lady would share with me many things she would not share with her family. She was honest with me about her frustrations with God when He did not seem to hear her prayers. She had been to a number of cancer clinics up and down the East Coast. Each place told her there was no hope for her. She had dedicated her life to teaching children and she could not understand why God did not help her fulfill that dream. She was not asking for healing just for her own personal benefit. She wanted to return to helping shape young lives. She could not understand why God did not give her that opportunity.

On one of my visits to her in the hospital as I was ready to leave I asked if I could offer a prayer. She turned her head to the wall away from me. I offered a short prayer and left. Later in the day I returned and asked her why she did not want to pray with me. She said she was angry with God. She could not understand why God did not love her. I told her that was ok to be angry with God. We are often angry with our earthly father and it is ok to be angry with Our Heavenly Father. He would surely understand.

I discussed with her the Bible Book of Job. Here was a perfect man. He had all the blessings anyone might desire. The Devil tried to convince God that the only reason Job believed and was faithful was because he had every possible human comfort. God gave the Devil the power to take every thing away from Job except his life. Through it all Job remained faithful. I am sure there were times Job must have questioned the faithfulness of God. But he never turned away from God. I told her that I believed that the reason we have the Book of Job in our Bible is to show that even good people can suffer. It also shows that God does not abandon those who suffer.

We discussed why we might be angry with God or at least disappointed in His responses to our prayers. It is hard to pray what I call a "Gethsemane Prayer." The night before Jesus Christ was crucified; He went upon the Mount of Olives and in a garden called Gethsemane, He prayed, "Father, if it is possible, let this cup pass from me, but nevertheless not as I will but as you will." (Matthew 26:36-42)

We can ask for whatever we wish, but we must leave the answers to a higher power. She was a middle age woman and could not understand why she had to die so young. Seldom did I have the answers to her questions, but we discussed the problems together.

Over the years I gathered information to help dying persons control the last days of their lives. Rather than just accept death, make it a meaningful experience for yourself and for those you leave. This is not always an easy effort. Too often the circumstances are too painful or too complicated for the patient to feel in control. Sometimes death comes unexpectedly and sudden as in an auto accident. Under those circumstances there is no time for choices. When you are given some time, use it according to your own wishes.

CHAPTER II
UNDERSTANDING YOUR ILLNESS

GET PRECISE INFORMATION

One of the first things one must do when faced with any illness that is diagnosed as terminal is to get accurate information. This may involve getting a second medical opinion, or it may mean to ask your present caregiver to give you more information. You need to know what are your options. Ask what treatments are available and what are their side effects?

Each cause of death brings with it alternative methods of treatment. Some forms of treatments will affect your quality and length of life and you may decide against them. Some illnesses offer no freedom of movement at all. However, if the treatment adds length to your life expectancy and/or more freedom of activity, you may decide to pay the price in the pain required.

There are no easy answers. Every illness is different. Every individual reacts in a different way from that of others.

If your prognosis is that you will live a few months or years, the treatment process may give you even more time. Treatment may increase the quality of life for your final days. There are also a variety of medications that can reduce pain and control the side effects of the illness. Find out what kind of pain management will be available. Your caregiver will be able to help you manage your pain. However, medication for pain may limit your participation in life around you. Inquire about choices available. Ask about side effects of the medication prescribed.

Ask what you might normally expect as to time left in your life. What stages would you possibly go through? What limitations might be placed upon you? What control can you have over your dying process? Answers to these questions will help you to better make decisions about your future. You need to know the possibilities of choices, if there are any.

No physician can predict with certainty what will happen in your future, but his/her experience will help to project some possibilities. One of the modern miracles is that many individuals are beating the odds on survival. Do not take any estimation as to time as final. Let it serve as a guide, but then determine to beat the odds.

Choose a support system

This is a time when you need at least one person with whom you can be totally honest about your situation. You may need more than one. You may need help in the various aspects of your life dealing with financial or other needs. You need at least one person with whom you can share your most private thoughts. There will be times when you will feel totally alone. Your negative thoughts may overwhelm you. These are times when you need an anchor, someone who will listen and help you find a positive response.

This person could be your spouse, a brother or sister. It could be a friend with whom you have shared other personal aspects of your life. It could be clergy person. It must be someone who could keep as sacred those things you do not wish to share with everyone. There will be times you will cry. There will be times you may curse your circumstances. These will be temporary outbursts and are best shared with a friend who can serve as an anchor for your attitude. You may not want to share your negative responses with everyone.

Our own thoughts are seldom complete until they have been expressed to another human mind. Sometimes, just talking out loud helps. However, it is much better to express your feelings and concerns to another person that can ask questions and give you feedback to help clarify your thoughts. It is not helpful to keep all of your fears and frustrations within your own mind. It is much better to have a safe unloading place.

Make sure you are clear on how much you want the larger circle of family and friends to know. If you wish to keep secret for a time the totality of your situation, you should be in control. What you choose to share will spread and cannot be taken back.

Some persons do not feel comfortable with a constant flow of sympathy and questions. You must remember you honor your friends by sharing your needs with them. Some will feel offended if they are excluded. Others may have difficulty carrying a burden of concern. Discuss all of this with your confidant(s). Map out a strategy. In all things put yourself in control of your last days. If at all possible, do not just sit back and let death run over you.

What medical resources are available?

The medical community has made tremendous advancements in many fields in recent years. Not every physician or hospital is prepared to give all patients the very latest technology. Frequently a doctor will refer his/her patient to a larger medical facility where they are better equipped to treat some medical needs. Sometimes the referral is made to a particular physician that has demonstrated special skills in caring for patients with this particular disease. Sometimes these are not good choices because of distance or cost. Again, evaluate and make your own choices.

Some medical centers excel in specific illnesses. Find out which is best for your own illness. U. S. News&World Report does an annual report on medical centers in the United States. The report is sub-divided according to illnesses. Medical Centers are rated from best to not so good for a particular illness.

One should try to pick the best institution closest to where you will spend most of your time. This will reduce travel time and cost. Another consideration will have to do with how far your family and friends will have to travel to visit you and support you emotionally.

As time passes and your physical condition worsens you will want your primary support persons to be able to visit you more frequently. You may have to make decisions as to where the majority of your treatment takes place to be more accessible to your family and friends. Again, put your own sense of needs first. Do not allow yourself to be forced into situations against your own **wishes** just to be able to please others.

INVENTORY OF YOUR LEGAL DOCUMENTS

This is a time when you need to take an inventory of all your assets and resources. Begin to gather vital papers that your survivors will need when you are gone. These are things that should be done by all persons in an ongoing schedule. It is most critical for the terminally ill. You may not have time to "do it later." Make sure your papers reflect your own desires.

Do an analysis of your financial situation. If you have savings, make a list as to location and amounts. If you have debts, make a list of amounts and the addresses of lenders and locations. Do you have business interests? Will your survivors know what to do regarding your relationship to your business concerns?

This is a good time to check your will and other legal papers. Our lives go through so many changes we do not always keep our legal papers updated. You will need to make sure your will expresses your present wishes. You may have acquired new assets or disposed of old assets that are not covered in your present will. If necessary, have your legal papers updated so that they will accomplish what you wish.

If you do not have a will you should consult an attorney. Make sure your wishes are carried out after you are no longer in charge. If you cannot afford an attorney, there are many kits you can buy to help you care for the basic legal needs. You need to make sure your legal documents are accepted in the state where you hold residence. You may wish to have a friend check with the Clerk of Court in your jurisdiction to make sure you are covered.

Take an inventory of the persons who are dependent upon you for financial support or other help. If you are a single parent with young children, what provisions have you made for these? You will need to make sure these needs will be cared for according to your wishes after you are no longer present to do it yourself. Check to see what other resources will be available to them when you are no longer there.

At some point you may want to take an inventory of things you may wish to give to others after your death. You may have guns, shop equipment, pictures, household items that you may want special persons to have. You may want to make a gift of these items while you live. It will prevent hard feelings when people begin to claim your items after you are not there.

When listing things you wish to give to others you may want to list separately those things you designate for others but that you wish to continue to use them during your lifetime. Again, here is a role for your trusted friend who can keep the list and deliver after your death.

A living will

A Living Will is a legal medical document recognized by hospitals and physicians. It expresses your desire on how you wish to be treated medically when you are no longer able to make those wishes known verbally. Most hospitals today will ask if you have one. If you do not have one they will offer to help you draft one. You must give instructions if you do not wish to be kept alive by heroic means when your body can no longer function by itself. Many people do not wish to be kept alive by the use of machines. If there is no hope of recovery, many do not wish to be kept in a vegetative state. The medical community is committed to doing all things possible to keep you alive. They will use every effort to keep you living as long as possible unless they are directed to do so by the patient's wishes as expressed in a Living Will. A Living Will enables you to make these choices ahead of time.

Durable Power of Attorney

There is also a medical document usually called "A Durable Power of Attorney." This document allows you to specify a trusted person with the power to override your Living Will if it is in your best interest. This person can act for you if the need arises and you are not able to act for yourself. You should discuss your intentions with your family members so that they will understand your wishes.

The value of a Durable Power of Attorney is that it is possible that there may be some new procedure not known at the time you wrote your Living Will that might help you. The field of medicine is constantly making dramatic discoveries and advancements. The person designated in your Durable Power of Attorney will be able to override your Living Will and give you that help. It also allows your chosen spokesperson to have access to your medical records if is in your best interest.

Insurance policies

Make sure your insurance policies have the correct beneficiary listed. Upon your death the proceeds of your life insurance policies will go to the person last registered with the insurance company as your beneficiary. There have been instances where the person named as beneficiary actually preceded the insured in death. Without a living designated beneficiary the distribution of funds is thrown into the courts to divide.

There are so many stories of men who died leaving a wife who knew nothing of the financial status of the family. Many lawsuits have been filed contesting a will that designated a beneficiary who was no longer in the picture. Relationships sometimes change. You must make sure your legal papers reflect those changes in a way agreeable to you.

Planning the immediate future

If you can keep on working for a time, how will your illness affect your work? It may require a visit with your boss or personnel person to evaluate your situation. If you cannot continue to work, what effect will that have on your income and health benefits? Can you take disability or medical retirement? What other resources do you have? If your health insurance is not adequate, what alternatives do you have?

If you are a veteran of one of the armed forces of the United States, you may want to visit a Veterans Hospital or a Veterans Representative to evaluate your alternatives there. The rules and provisions for care are constantly changing. It is best to check the latest provisions and availability. This is a time you may want your state and/or federal political representatives to check for you.

Most hospitals also have a resident Social Worker to help patients evaluate their medical resources. These persons can help you with determine the availability of home healthcare when you are not hospitalized. You may need some kind of special medical equipment. The social worker can help you find the proper resource.

Hospice

Hospice combines well-trained medical personnel with trained volunteers who bring their heart into their work as well as their head. This ministry is available at most hospitals for those that have been told they have six-months or less to live and are referred by a physician.

Hospice has available registered nurses that are trained to meet any emergency in the hospital or in the home of the patient. Most Hospices have a bereavement coordinator to work with the patient and family to be able to deal with the transition from this life to the next.

When the patient is admitted to Hospice in the hospital, they are placed in special rooms in an environment that encourages family participation. A nurse, a social worker, and volunteers make regular visits when the patient is in the home.

HOME CARE VISITING NURSE

Many communities have a program whereby a trained nurse will come to the home to provide medical care for sick persons. These nurses can administer medication prescribed by a physician and oversee the medical care received in the home. Many patients come home from the hospital still having drainage tubes, feeding tubes and special bandages that must be treated with great care. As indicated above, the Social Worker in the hospital can make the arrangements for this care.

ACCEPT HELP FROM CARING FAMILY AND FRIENDS

While we are well we are hesitant to ask for or to receive help from others. Too often we see it as a sign of weakness. We are afraid to impose on others for our own comfort. This is an opportunity to give those who care about you an opportunity to do something good for you. Your closest friend or loved one may hesitate to be asked to help. When you ask for and receive help you offer a blessing to the caregiver. You give more than you receive. In receiving you give a blessing. The Scripture challenge is to "ask and you will receive." (Matthew 7:7)

CHAPTER III

FACE YOUR ENEMY

Know your enemy

As indicated above, you must decide how much you want to know about your illness. Sometimes the full picture is too frightening. It may be better to know just the basic facts. You have a right to know what you want to know. You may choose to have a private consultation with your physician. You may then choose what you want to share with others about your illness.

You may want to ask your primary medical caregiver to give you some literature. Most medical facilities have a wide range of literature that they will gladly make available to you. Ask a nurse or other health care person for help and they will guide you.

You may also want to ask for the names of others that are in the same process of death, as are you. Sometimes you can learn more about pain, limitations and body functions from another patient than from a caregiver. You may be able to help each other as you share your own experiences. You must remember that no two persons react in the same way to the same disease. There will be many similarities and some differences. The fellowship of walking together, even if by phone, is often very comforting.

It can also be helpful to visit with a family who has recently lost a family member to that disease. This can be a good or bad choice. Some families have wonderful memories of the last days their loved one spent with them. Others may only remember the pain and will paint a dark picture. Through this experience you might be able to better understand the choices that you have.

Ask selected friends to help you research your illness. There is much on the Internet regarding illnesses. WebMD web site offers much information. Be careful about accepting everything on the Internet as absolute truth. These are opinions of various individuals. The articles are informative, but are not substitutes for opinions of your own personal physician.

Libraries have many books describing in great detail the disease, treatment, and limitations your disease brings. Most medical centers have booklets that are very helpful. Duke Medical Center in Durham, North Carolina has a clinic for each disease or illness and in that area they have a resource center with much information to help understand your problem. Often there is a volunteer present in the resource center to help you find the particular information you need.

Most diseases take a variety of forms and attack many parts of the human body. One thing you will learn is that "everyone is different." Just because you find one case history of your disease does not mean your own journey will be just like that one. However, you can learn that there are many facets of how that disease attacks the human body and life.

Recognize your personal limitations

Take inventory of your physical limitations. What limitations do you already have? Are you able to go where you want to go under your own power? Will you be able to drive yourself where you want to go? Can you read clearly? How about your appetite? Find out what kind of diet will give you the best life style and longest life. Ask about exercises that might help. Chart a course for yourself. In so far as is possible, plan your activities within your possibilities, as you understand them. Your physician will be able to help you choose activities that will help and not harm. Most medical facilities have a Physical Therapist available to help you with exercise possibilities.

You probably will have to make many adjustments. You will find many excuses not to put forth the effort. Caring friends and family will give you much advice about what might help you. But, you should be in charge. It may seem easier to just quit. You will be tempted to take what appears to be an easier course. In the long run you will find that you are better off if you fight your limitations. Do not over extend, but do not quit! Every effort you put forth will buy you a better life.

The journey is easier if you do not have to travel alone. If you have a spouse or other significant person let this person walk with you. As time passes it will become increasingly more important to have someone near to do those things you cannot do alone. Times will come when you will need a confidant with whom you can share your fears and frustrations. When you are down, it helps to have someone to lift your spirits up.

Through much of our lives we are too busy to have much quality time with those who are closest to us. Now, when you have come to the possible ending of your days, there is time. Put forth an effort to spend time with those whom you love that will give meaning to your relationship. As pointed out earlier, make these last days of your life the most meaningful of all. I like to think that the last days serve as a picture frame around all the rest of our lives. Make them beautiful.

Don't give up too easily

One of the most powerful healing tools available to you is your own positive attitude. At any given moment in our lives there are positive and negative possibilities as to how we might react to any given situation. We can decide which we shall choose. In every flower garden there are good and bad seeds. We decide which we shall water. Both are there, but we decide which shall get our primary attention. With your attitude you can create dark pictures of your future or you can reach for rays of hope. This is not always easy to do, but it is always rewarding. There is victory when you can live your last days on a positive note, even when you do not overcome.

This is especially true of individuals who have been diagnosed with a terminal illness. No matter what our disease, we usually have known of someone who has died of that very disease. Too often we remember the tragic stories but do not remember the success stories. Today there are many survivors. Many of the illnesses, which in the past were seen as a death sentence, now can boast of many survivors. Those who overcome, or at least have extended their time, have a tendency to fall back into the normal stream of life and we forget their battle and their successes.

The point is, the medical community cannot predict with certainty how long a particular patient will live. They can give you the best of their experience with past patients. They will be quick to tell you that each human body is an entity unto itself. There are so many variables. Your attitude and the environment in which your healing takes place will alter the manner in which your body will respond to treatment. We have pointed out before that each person is different when it comes to physical responses. Our bodies have traveled our own personal past. Each body has its own measure of strength. But, there are many human similarities.

New medicines and new medical procedures are being developed every day. You may be the beginning of a new understanding of your disease. Miracles still happen! At this point I have overcome Pancreatic Cancer. I have had **eight** six months reports of being free of Pancreatic cancer. I am an example of how God still uses the medical community to perform miracle healing. Even if you do not achieve total healing you can buy longer life and/or greater mobility.

FACE YOUR ENEMY WITH A POSITIVE MIND

Let me emphasize again how important it is that you keep a positive mind as you face your enemy. If the patient gives up without a positive effort, the medical community is severely handicapped in its effort to help. You must decide that you will overcome. You can at least give yourself a better quality of life for the days you have.

I remember serving for a short time toward the end of the Korean War as a Navy Chaplain at the Oak Knoll Navy Hospital in Oakland, California. This hospital specialized in taking care of the young men who had lost legs and/or arms in the Korean War. I noticed how the attitude of the patient had so much to do with the speed with which they adapted to their new circumstances.

For all of these young men the rest of their days were drastically altered. Some began quickly to adopt a survivor attitude. They decided to use what future they had to build a new life. Others took much longer because they did not try at first. They spent much longer time in the hospital. Still others became permanent patients and retreated inside themselves and shut the world out. I concluded that, to some degree at least; our own will power can influence the quality of our days.

Your disease may place many limitations upon you. You may be limited in where you must live and limited in your freedom of movement. Only you have the final say about your attitude. In your mind you can be as free as you choose to be. Sometimes the pain and frustration seem as insurmountable walls. Your disease and the pain it causes can become a prison. With a negative attitude you can create a prison for yourself, if you choose to do so. With a positive attitude you can create an atmosphere of victory around you. Your positive attitude can have a healing effect on others around you. It is not too hard to have a positive attitude, but to keep it requires constant effort.

Your caregiver and your loved ones around you may try to protect you by making you their prisoner. Out of their love for you they will do everything possible to help you. It can be done as far as the physical body. But, you can be free in your mind and in your soul. You can soar to heights of imagination beyond any wall of limitation.

In so far as is possible, use the freedom of your mind to organize your activities and your involvement in your treatment. When you have decided to take control of your circumstances, you will have begun to set yourself free. This does not mean that you do not need help from your caregiver and others. It means that you will make the final decision after carefully considering the options presented to you.

You will find that others who care greatly about you may not always agree with your choices. They may see a different option, which they consider to be better for you. They may be afraid you may harm yourself by too much exertion. But, you will feel better in the long run if you feel you can make your own choices.

CHAPTER IV

RELIGIOUS CONCERNS

Much has been written about death. Most of what has been written is to tell the story of someone who died. Death has many faces. It is the most unpredictable event in our lives. It comes to persons of all ages and in the midst of all kinds of circumstances. It matters not how busy we are or how vital our continued effort might be. Death takes the high and the lowly in life. No one is beyond the claims of death. At some point it is certain that we shall all die.

Even a casual study of the history of the human race reveals that death has been a reality in every civilization and culture. Each civilization developed its own concept of the meaning of death. There are at least two beliefs that were present in every civilization from the beginning of creation. One had to do with the reality of death and the existence beyond death. Mankind has always believed that the dead person would continue to exist in some form, in some place, beyond the grave.

Connected with this belief of existence beyond the grave was the development of religions. Mankind has always been religious. This does not mean that their idea of religion would fit into any of our religious groups of the modern day. It does mean that they believed that there was a non-human power outside their person that in some way had control over their destiny. Sometimes elaborate ceremonies were developed to win the favor of that divine power. Special individuals were designated to be a specialist in dealing with this power. These clergy type persons yielded great power in their communities and tribes.

Often it was believed that there were many special deities. In some cultures each deity was believed to control only certain aspects of life. The main concern of this writing is to point out that death has been a part of life from the beginning and that there has always been a belief in existence beyond death. Every past civilization has believed in a supreme power and life beyond the grave. Today, in every culture, these two concepts still shape the cultures of our day.

It is important to ask why mankind ever felt a need for a religious belief and a concept of existence beyond the grave? In every civilization there is evidence of an effort to know and appease the creator. It is more than just a feeling that a life so vital here could not cease to exist completely at death. In most modern western religions there is a belief that God created mankind. God may be called God or Allah. It is also believed that

God created mankind in His own image. This does not mean mankind was created to look like God in a physical form. It does mean that God placed within each human individual something that would be eternal and therefore never cease to exist. Many call this eternal part a soul. This "soul" also was created to seek to know its Creator.

It should be recognized that there are those who do not believe in a divine creation of the universe and/or life. They hold to some theory as to the origin of life and the universe. These are called evolutionists. These evolutionists have no theory as to the origin of the material from which the universe evolved. Nor do they have a theory as to the source of the power that set in motion the evolution process. However, they have done much to help us understand how the natural world works.

Religious people have helped us to understand the source of the universe. The Judeo-Christian religions deal primarily with the source of life and the universe. The Scriptures make no effort to explain the process of change taking place in our world and universe. There is no effort in Scripture to explain how God created life and the universe. The primary concern of Scripture is getting to know the Creator, to live a peaceful life here and making appropriate preparation for our existence beyond the grave.

The purpose of this writing is to help each person take an inventory of their own life and to make such preparations for their own death as they might choose. There are religious concerns to be addressed as death approaches. Each individual must decide just how they will face these concerns. If you are a religious person, it is time to review your own beliefs about life and death. If you have a relationship with an established religion you may want to consult with someone within that religion to help you to deal with the questions about death and life beyond the grave.

If you have no established relationship with a religious group, you may want to talk to trusted friends about their concepts. You need not be forced into any concept held by others. Every human person is free to make his or her own religious decisions. You must feel free in whatever decisions you make. It is important to most people to feel prepared for life beyond the grave. It is of immense comfort to the family and friends you leave behind to believe that you were prepared to die and to face existence beyond the grave.

Even if you are anti-religious, you should explore all sides of the issue. The religious teachings of the western world require that an individual make some sort of positive decision regarding life beyond the grave. The Christian religion as practiced by most churches requires a positive faith in Jesus Christ.

The way in which this positive faith is registered varies among the various groups, but the basic requirement, if you want life and peace beyond death you must believe that Jesus Christ is a real person. You need to believe that the New Testament account of the life and death of Jesus is true. Faith in the fact that the death of Jesus on the cross was payment for the sins of all believers removes the penalty for sin from all believers. There is a choice of life or death beyond the grave. Life is possible through faith in Jesus Christ. If no positive decision is made, then death or Hell is the destiny. All human persons will exist beyond the grave in some place. Where and how is determined by decisions made prior to death.

There is no argument needed to prove that we are all imperfect persons. No human being has ever lived without making some errors in life. There has never been a perfect society at any point in history.

The nature of mankind has been the same throughout history. There have always been wars. There are always those who prey upon others for their survival. Even the best among us fail in some ways. We are constantly discovering flaws in past heroes.

Even if it were possible to find one individual who never did anything wrong, the question then is did they do all the good things that could have been done. Did they take care of all the poor, sick, etc. during their lifetime?

Sin is both positive and negative. It involves doing wrong things and also failure to do good things. That is why Scripture teach that all are sinners. (Romans 3:10, 23; 6:23) It was the sinful nature of mankind that Jesus came to remove. (John 3:16-21) The Scriptures also teach that we are not able to do enough good in our own behalf to cancel out all sin from our lives. (Ephesians 2:8-10) Jesus Christ, being God in human form, took our place on the cross and made the only acceptable eternal sacrifice for sin. It is by faith in Him and His death and resurrection that we have continued access to God in this life and beyond the grave.

CHAPTER V
MAKING A FINAL STATEMENT

Having been diagnosed as a terminal patient is a frightening experience to say the least. There is, however, a positive side to the event. Each person is given the hope of some time before death will take place. It is similar to the two-minute warning that professional football players get. It is a statement that the game is almost over and you have this limited time to do something to change the outcome. The referee blows his whistle and says, in effect, "Fellows the game is almost over. You see what the score is now. I am giving you a set time of two minutes to do what you can to change the outcome of the game. It can be a whole new ballgame. It is up to you."

So many persons die without a warning that the end is near. People who die in car accidents are often killed without even a moment to understand what is happening. Many who have fatal heart attacks have no moments to make final arrangements for their end.

Each person who is informed that they have a medical condition that will take their life in a short time should give thanks for that possible time, no matter how short it might be. It is important to use that time in a way that will give hope and a sense of purpose to others that may experience a terminal illness in the future. These days, or years, can be the most meaningful of all that has gone before. Many have made a greater impact with their lives in those final days than all the other days and years in the past. People listen and take note of every effort made in this time.

We cannot be expected to give thanks for our coming death, but we can give thanks for the time to prepare. We have been blessed with something money cannot buy. The question is how shall we use it?

With the end of life more clearly in focus, it is time to bring closure in every area of life. It is time to take an inventory of the various areas of the past. This inventory would include much of what has already been addressed. In addition to financial, a will, advance directives relative to medical treatment, it is necessary to look at human relationships. Are there significant persons from whom you have been alienated, for whatever reason? Ask yourself if you would feel better if you mended those relationships before you die? Are there special persons who have blessed your life? Now is the time to let them know.

Do not be afraid to make the first step. Death will be much more peaceful if you are at peace with those persons who are important to you.

FUNERAL AND BURIAL.

If you have not already made pre-arrangements for your funeral, you may want to do so now. Not everyone feels the need to give instructions regarding their own funeral and place of burial. If you have any special feelings you should put them in writing or share them with your family. The average funeral involves the writing of an obituary, music to be played or sung, and choice of pallbearers. You may want to make these choices yourself. There is also a choice of where you will be buried. If you have not made a pre-arrangement, you may at least now want to make your wishes known. Remember that the funeral is really for those you leave behind. What would you like to be included in the funeral service? This is your last opportunity to offer public support to your family and friends. They will be blessed if they believe they are doing what you would choose.

More and more people are opting for cremation instead of normal burial. One of the primary reasons for choosing cremation is the high cost of a customary funeral and burial site. With cremation you have a wide range of choices. Most cemeteries have a Columbarium or other facilities for display of urns containing the ashes of deceased individuals. The cost is far less.

If you are a veteran of the armed forces of the United States you may qualify to be buried in the Arlington National Cemetery. If you have been the recipient of certain high medals you may be interred in the ground in a separate burial plot with a marker. If you choose, your spouse may be interred with you. Both of you will occupy the same space. If you have not been the recipient of one of the higher medals your cremated remains may be interred in the Columbarium there in Arlington National Cemetery.

The least expensive funeral arrangements would be to request immediate cremation upon death. Then have a memorial service later. This would not require a casket for viewing. It would not require the expense of paying for the use of a funeral home and staff. There are many Cremation Societies and cemeteries that will come to the place of death and remove the body for cremation. They will assist in the necessary paperwork required at death.

A memorial service can be held in a local church or other facility where the cost will be minimal or none at all. You can leave instructions as to how this might be conducted.

Not everyone feels comfortable with cremation. Many desire the traditional funeral arrangements. It is helpful if each person would express his/her desires long before the time of need. Death is an emotional experience for all concerned. It is very easy for families to overspend trying to show love and appreciation for the deceased. It is hard to remember that funerals are for the benefit of the living not the dead. It brings closure and gives opportunity to verbalize feelings regarding the deceased. It is better if these decisions are made before required. Each funeral home will assist in making choices.

How much do you want to decide?

Many people have very definite ideas as to where they wish to be buried. Some who wish to be cremated also have specific ideas where they would like their ashes interred or scattered. Some want their ashes scattered in the mountains, at sea, or near a meaningful place.

If you have specific desires regarding your funeral and/or place of final resting-place, you should express them clearly in writing or to the person who will be in charge of your final things. If you have no specific wishes, you may choose to let your family decide.

Making your final statement.

What you do in the time between your diagnosis as a terminal patient and the day of your death is your final statement about life. It will demonstrate, as nothing else can your real beliefs about your family and friends. It also will show your true religious beliefs. Your attitude, words and deeds will almost be as if they were carved in stone.

You can touch those whom you love in many very special ways that they will remember for their lifetime. Your words will ring true to all that hear or read. *You will not get a second chance to have a last chance.*

Having been told that you have a limited number of months or years to live gives you the opportunity to make a statement about yourself and your view of life in a very special way. Take charge of your life. Within your physical limitations, reach out to those who have blessed your life. Help them to be prepared for the time you will no longer be there. Make your going from this life a loving and meaningful experience for all persons in your life.

This is your life! Live it in your way. Use every resource available to help you live as long as possible and with as much dignity and meaning possible. You have a special given opportunity. Live it with purpose. Give it a try!

APPENDIX A

MY FAITH HAS ANCHORS

Dr. Calvin E. Rains, Sr.

What sustains your faith when things continue to go bad? Most religious messages today seem to promise that if you will just have faith, everything will go well for you. You will earn more money and you will be healthy.

I believe it is true that if you put your trust in Jesus Christ things will go better in your life. But, how can your faith sustain you if your world begins to fall apart. How can you still trust when pain fills your every day?

We need a faith that is anchored in certain things that do not fade. My salvation is based in part on facts and part faith. There are some things we know as historical facts. We know that the world and universe came into being at sometime from some source. Our Evolutionist

Scientists have helped us to better understand how life and the universe evolved from one stage to another. Evolutionists deal with the **process** of evolution. They have no explanation of the **source** of the universe. I know of no ***theory*** of the source of the matter from which things evolved. Neither do they have a theory of the source of the energy that set in motion the evolutionary process, which they study.

The Bible has little to say about the **process** of change in our world. However, in the first eleven chapters of Genesis God introduces Himself to mankind as the **source** of life and all that is. When Yahweh spoke to Moses at the burning bush He gave Moses a basis for faith in God as Creator. He also introduced Moses to an explanation for the moral condition of mankind and to His plan for the redemption of mankind.

You can study the history of the human race and you will find certain constants. Mankind has always been religious. There is something within the makeup of man that tells him that there is a power outside him that in someway has control of man's destiny.

Second, mankind has always believed in an existence beyond death. Man has often formed his own deities and explanation of existence beyond death. Mankind has always believed in good and evil. Evil persons would be punished beyond the grave and good persons would be rewarded.

NOW, from where did these concepts originate? How is it possible that for century after century the moral nature of man stayed the same? Why has there never been a perfect generation that had no poor, no wars, but only peace? If we are only natural human beings, it looks like some would have gotten it right somewhere on this globe. History records that no matter where mankind lived on the face of the world, isolated or together, he has been the same moral person.

Some believers have a problem with the story of creation as reported to Moses by God Himself. I have no problem at all. I believe the scientific explanation that it took millions of years for the world and universe, as we know it to reach its present state. You might say, "The Bible says it took only six days." That is right, I believe the Bible completely. The problem is that the six days of creation took place in eternity. They were six days of God's time. Mankind had not yet sinned. When Adam and Eve were put out of the Garden they entered the realm of time. When we die and enter into the presence of Our Lord we will enter His time, which is eternal. When Jesus comes again, time will be no more. You have time from the moment Adam and Eve sinned until Jesus comes again.

These are some of the pillars of fact that help my faith when things go bad. Believing the facts will not save you. However they serve as a window through which you can better see the Jesus of the New Testament. We are saved by faith through the grace of God. Our sins are removed by Faith in Jesus and His redeeming work on the cross. His resurrection gave proof of His life and death. Matthew 28:6 gives us a clue to how our salvation takes place. The angel told the women who were first to come to the empty tomb that Jesus was risen. The Greek for the word "risen" is an aorist passive, which means, "He has been raised." The power that brought Jesus alive from the tomb did not originate in the tomb. It did not originate in the dead body of Jesus. The power that brought Our Savior back to life again came from the throne of God. So is with my salvation. The power to redeem me did not come from within me. It did not come from the church of my praying friends. The power that redeemed my soul came from the throne of God where my Lord Jesus sits today.

SO, My faith is based on Scripture and is strengthened by the historical facts of the history of man. Sometimes it is hard to feel the presence of my Lord, and then I look at the world around me and remember how it all happened. I know I can trust the word of my Lord concerning what will happen from here on into eternity.

How is your life anchored? What do you believe about existence beyond death? Are you prepared to face your concepts? God has demonstrated His love for mankind. He offers complete forgiveness of sin through faith in Jesus Christ. "God so loved the world that He gave His only begotten Son that whoever believes in Him shall have everlasting life." John 3:16 There is my anchor as I face the storms of life and death.

APPENDIX B

WHY THIS PAIN?

Dr. Calvin E. Rains, Sr.

Within the last few days I have visited both my local Doctor and Duke Medical Center. It has been one year since I started this journey with Pancreatic Cancer. In the process I have lost 50 pounds of weight and a little over four inches in height. My back is bowed and my pace has slowed, but I have not quit. An elderly ex-mayor of Martinsville talked with me the other day when I was walking in the mall. He said people look at what I have been through the last three years: two triple bypass surgeries and a whipple procedure surgery for cancer, and people have called me "a Tough Old Bird."

I am so grateful to still be alive and able to get out among people. I am grateful for the time with my wife of 54 years and children and granddaughters (5). But I am in agonizing pain every morning. The worst time of my day is getting out of bed and getting dressed. My back hurts so I have difficulty taking a step. It usually takes until noon to be able to walk with any success. But, I know that I cannot quit!

It is at times like these I question my God. Why do I have this pain and why is it so severe? I served my Lord for 54 years: I have preached in three foreign countries, I spent a year as chaplain with the Marine Infantry at the end of the Korean War, and have served churches in five states. Why do I now suffer so? Am I being punished for some sin I have not confessed? Am I being punished for some service I did not render? WHY? I believe that God does not cause pain. He is there within our experience. I also know we can bring pain and difficulty on ourselves through bad choices. Some cancer is a result of bad habits earlier in life. At this time no one knows what causes Pancreatic Cancer. Why then do I have this pain?

Let me say I have concluded that this pain is my new area of ministry. I am now given a new way of ministering to people. A young man just this day said, "you are an inspiration to us all." I get replies from my Medical Report telling me how my reports on journey is a help to their ministry to other people.

The Book of Job is a new inspiration to me. Job was a perfect man (I am not) and yet he lost everything: family and wealth. His best friends pointed him out in derision. Job never quit! He never weakened in his faith in God. The Book of Job is in our Bible to show that good and obedient people can suffer also.

I have spent long hours in conversation with my Lord. I have analyzed my past mistakes and questioned myself if I have made adequate confession and adjustments in my efforts. I have never claimed, nor believed that I was holy, except that I belong to God. I have tried to be like Jesus since I was seventeen years old. I am now almost 78 years of age. I am ready to stand before Jesus. I accept this new opportunity of ministry. I will try to share my faith through keeping on keeping on.

I do not accept this pain and limitation as punishment. I accept it as an opportunity to minister to others who must walk this path or to those who have loved ones who suffer. Some may remember an attachment in the past, which asked if this journey was "A Test or Opportunity." I accept this as a new opportunity. I have found opportunities all along my path. God has also planted angels along my path to help me every day. God bless you as you and may God help you in every difficult moment.

When things go wrong let us analyze it to see what corrections we have to make and then accept it as an opportunity to grow in our faith. Our Lord did not quit when He saw that only the cross lay ahead for Him. Find a way of being a blessing to those around you. God Bless you.

ABOUT THE AUTHOR

Rev. Dr. Calvin E. Rains, Sr. holds four earned degrees from three institutions of higher learning. He has studied the Scriptures in the original languages of Hebrew and Greek.

He served **58** years as a Baptist minister. He retired because he was diagnosed with Pancreatic Cancer and the chemotherapy treatment. He served in WWII as a Navy Carrier based Fighter Pilot. He saw action against Japan. He was wounded once and received the Purple Heart and the Air Medal.

After WWII he became a minister. When the Korean War began, he felt the men needed a minister with them. Rev. Rains returned to active Navy Service as a Navy Chaplain. He served various Navy Bases and as a Chaplain with the U. S. Marines in Korea. While serving as a Chaplain he also served as a Prison Chaplain and Counselor. He also served in a Navy Hospital counseling young men who had lost arms, legs, etc in Korea to help them adjust to a new future.

He has had extensive service with HOSPICE dealing with terminally ill persons and CONTACT, a 24-hour telephone crisis ministry.

Rev. Rains has overcome Pancreatic Cancer and Prostate Cancer and he continues to minister to others who have been diagnosed as a terminal patient.